This library edition published in 2020 by Walter Foster Jr.,
an imprint of The Quarto Group
26391 Crown Valley Parkway, Suite 220
Mission Viejo, CA 92691, USA.

Distributed in the United States and Canada by
Lerner Publisher Services
241 First Avenue North
Minneapolis, MN 55401 U.S.A.
www.lernerbooks.com

First Library Edition

Library of Congress Cataloging-in-Publication Data

Title: Learn to draw Marvel Spider-Man.
Description: First library edition. | Mission Viejo, CA : Walter Foster Jr.,
     an imprint of The Quarto Group, 2020. | Audience: Ages: 6+. | Audience:
     Grades: 4-6.
Identifiers: LCCN 2019017164 | ISBN 9781600588327 (hardcover)
Subjects: LCSH: Superheroes in art--Juvenile literature. | Spider-Man
     (Fictitious character)--Juvenile literature. | Cartoon characters in
     art--Juvenile literature. | Drawing--Technique--Juvenile literature.
Classification: LCC NC1764.8.H47 L43 2020 | DDC 741.5/6--dc23 LC record available at
https://lccn.loc.gov/2019017164

Printed in USA
9 8 7 6 5 4 3 2 1

FSC
www.fsc.org
MIX
Paper from
responsible sources
FSC® C008080

TABLE OF CONTENTS

THE STORY OF SPIDER-MAN

Peter Parker was just a baby when his parents, who were U.S. government spies, died in a plane crash. He was raised by his Uncle Ben and Ant May. Peter was smart, especially when it came to science, but he was shy and often bullied at Midtown High School.

When he was 15, Peter attended a public science exhibit. While there, a radioactive spider bit him on the hand, and the bite gave him the spider's abilities of strength, agility, and the ability to cling to almost any surface. He also gained a Spider-Sense that warned him that danger was nearby. He used his intelligence to create artificial web-shooters that attached to his wrists.

Peter created a costume so he could enter a wrestling contest and win some money. At the wrestling gig, he allowed a burglar to escape with some stolen money, even though he could of easily stopped him. A few days later, Peter's Uncle Ben was shot and killed by this same burglar. Consumed with guilt, Peter realized at last that with great power comes great responsibility, just as his uncle had once said.

To help his Aunt May pay the bills, Peter began selling photos of himself as Spider-Man to the *Daily Bugle* newspaper. Unfortunately, the newspaper claimed Spider-Man was a menace, and the Super Hero was feared by the public. Things weren't much better for Peter at school. Flash Thompson and other kids called him "Puny Parker."

In addition to his personal problems, Spider-Man soon found himself having to save the city from many dangerous characters, including the Chameleon, the Tinkerer, the Vulture, Doctor Octopus, Lizard, the Sandman, the Green Goblin, and more.

TOOLS & MATERIALS

You need to gather only a few simple art supplies before you begin. Start with a drawing pencil and an eraser. Make sure you also have a pencil sharpener and a ruler. To add color to your drawings, use markers, colored pencils, crayons, watercolors, or acrylic paint. The choice is yours!

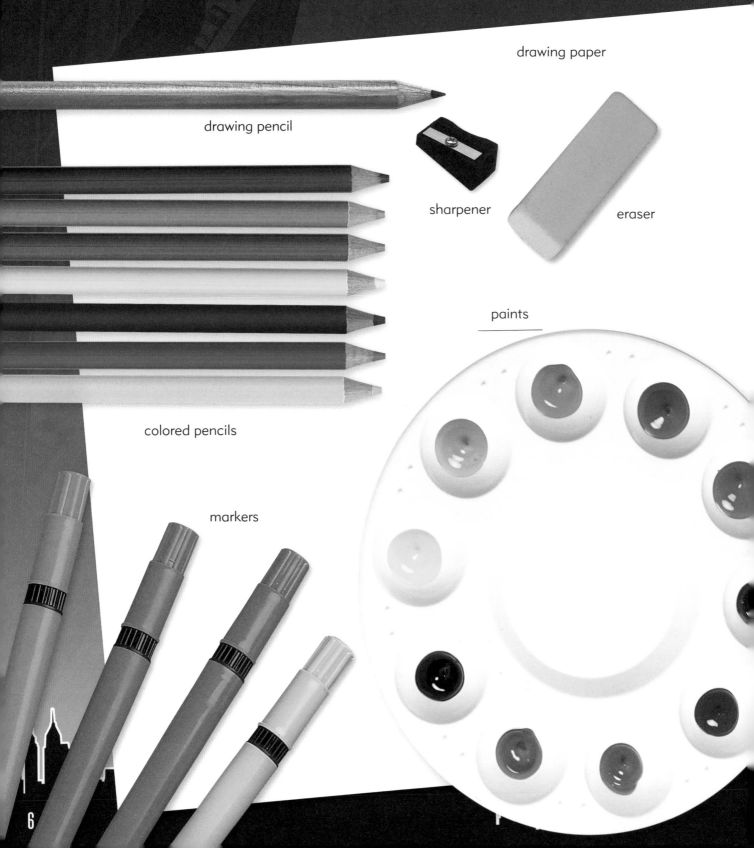

drawing paper

drawing pencil

sharpener

eraser

colored pencils

paints

markers

paintbrushes

BASIC SHAPES DRAWING METHOD

When using the step-by-step drawing method,
you will begin by drawing very basic shapes,
such as lines and circles.

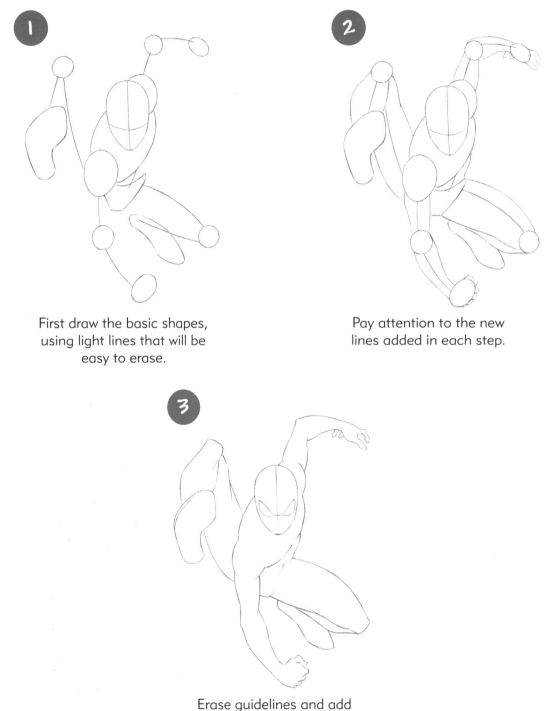

1 First draw the basic shapes, using light lines that will be easy to erase.

2 Pay attention to the new lines added in each step.

3 Erase guidelines and add more detail.

4

5

In each new step, add
more defining lines.

Take your time adding detail and
copying what you see.

6

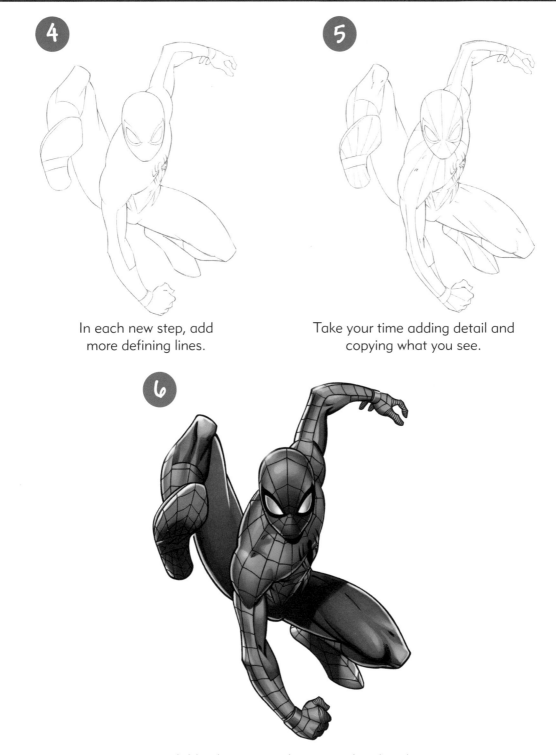

Add color to your drawing with colored
pencils, markers, paints, or crayons!

SPIDER-MAN ANATOMY

Spider-Man is not overly muscular, like a lot of Super Heroes.
His strength comes from his super spider powers, not bulky muscles.

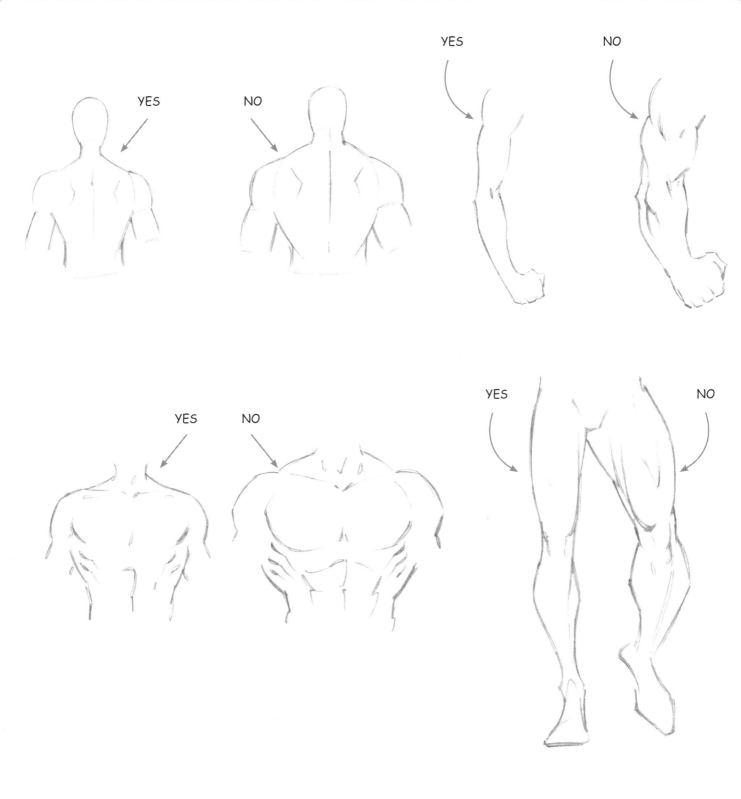

When drawing Spider-Man, use the eyes to show emotion. You don't have a mouth or facial muscles to draw, so the only way to show what he's thinking is through subtle changes in the mask's eye shapes. Note that in profile, Spider-Man's nose is visible. In a three-quarter view, the bulge of his ears is visible.

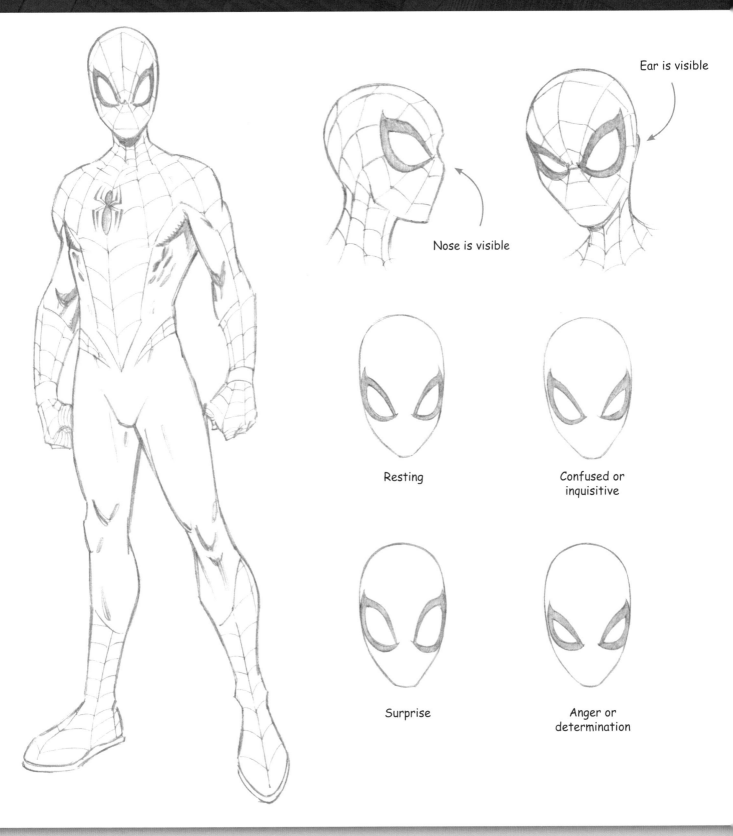

Ear is visible

Nose is visible

Resting

Confused or inquisitive

Surprise

Anger or determination

INKING TECHNIQUES

When inking, use different line weights and textures
to define the shapes and the image as a whole.

Fill in entire shapes in certain areas to emphasize the shadows.
To show changes from solid black shadows to lighter areas, use
hatching, crosshatching, or "feathered" brushstrokes or pen strokes.

Filled in area

Thin line weight

Thick line weight

COLORING TECHNIQUES

You can color your drawings any way you'd like,
using colored pencils, markers, or paints.

You can color Spider-Man using one shade of red and one of blue, and he will definitely look like Spider-Man. But if you want to take coloring to the next level, pay more attention to shadows and highlights.

See how in the second example, Spider-Man looks more three-dimensional? This is because the lighter and darker areas bring out Spider-Man's form.

SPIDER-MAN

Bitten by a radioactive spider, high school student Peter Parker gains the speed, strength, and powers of a spider. Adopting the name Spider-Man, Peter hopes to start a wrestling career using his new abilities. But taught that with great power comes great responsibility, Spidey instead vows to use his powers to help people.

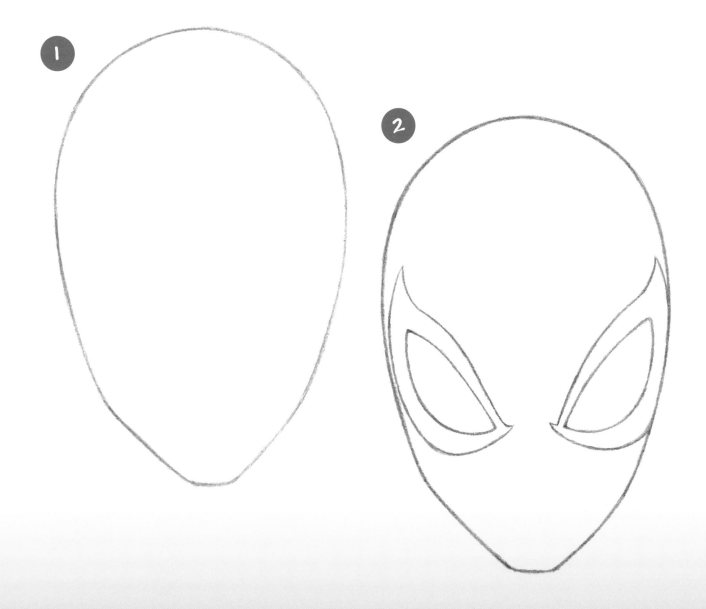

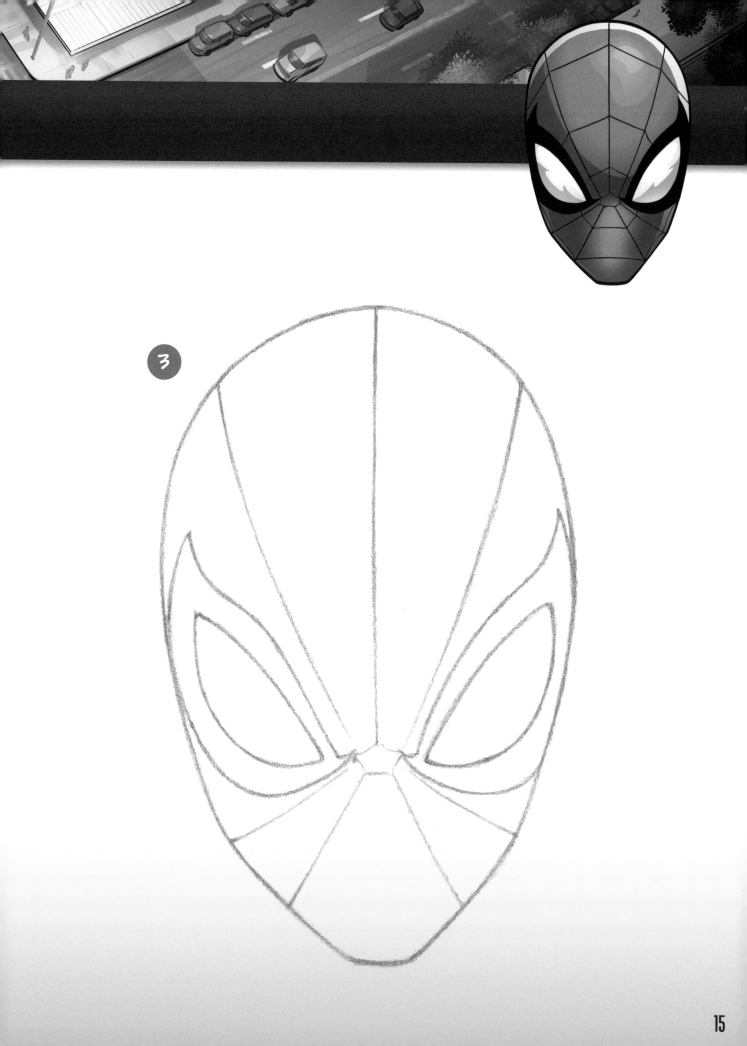

3

5

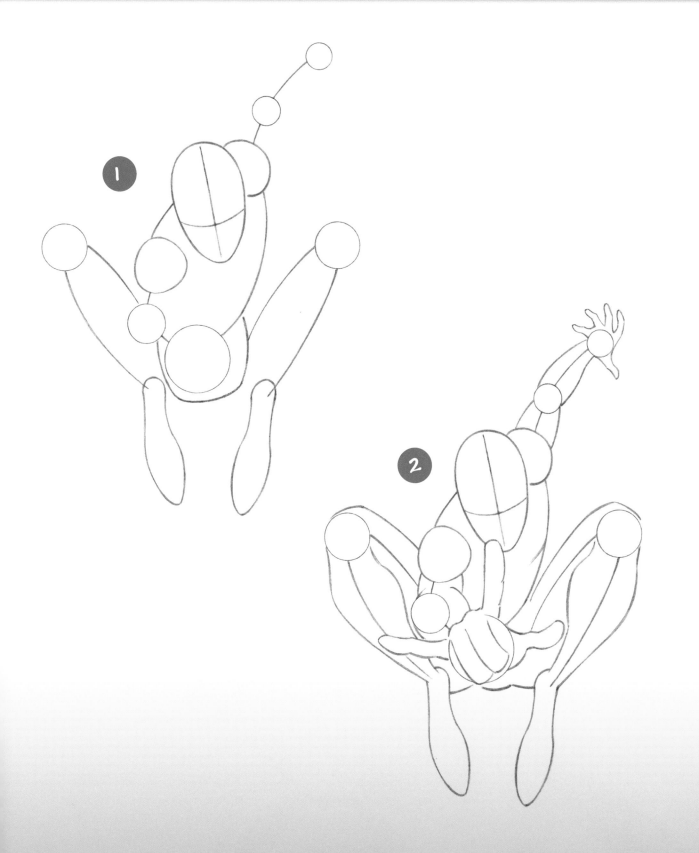

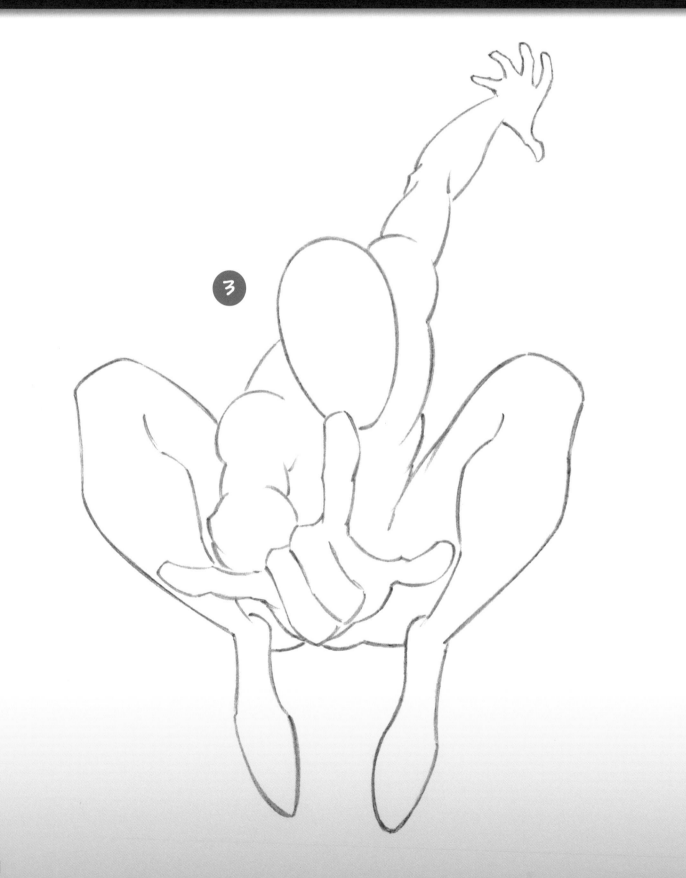

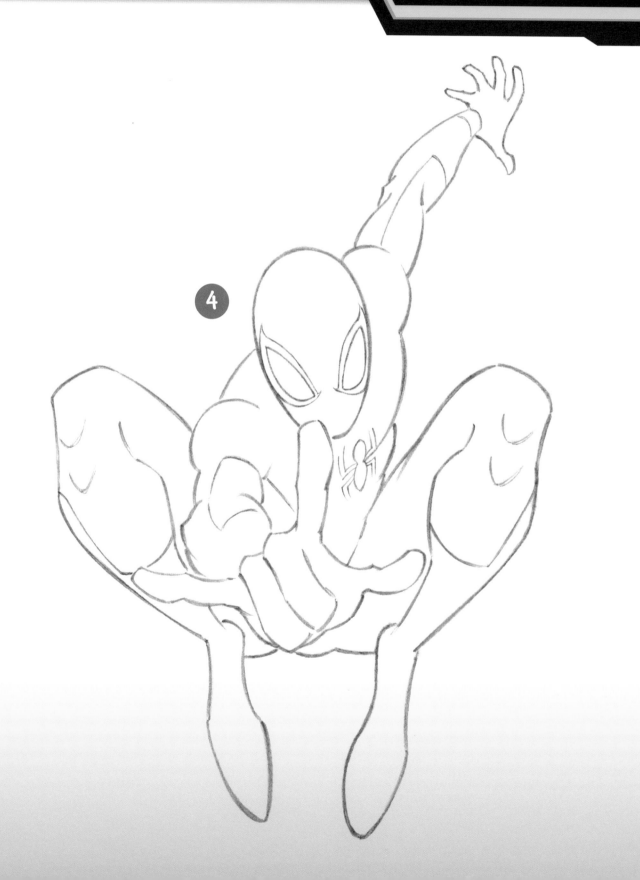

Spider-Man's first appearance is in
Amazing Fantasy #15,
the last issue of *Amazing Fantasy*,
published in 1962.

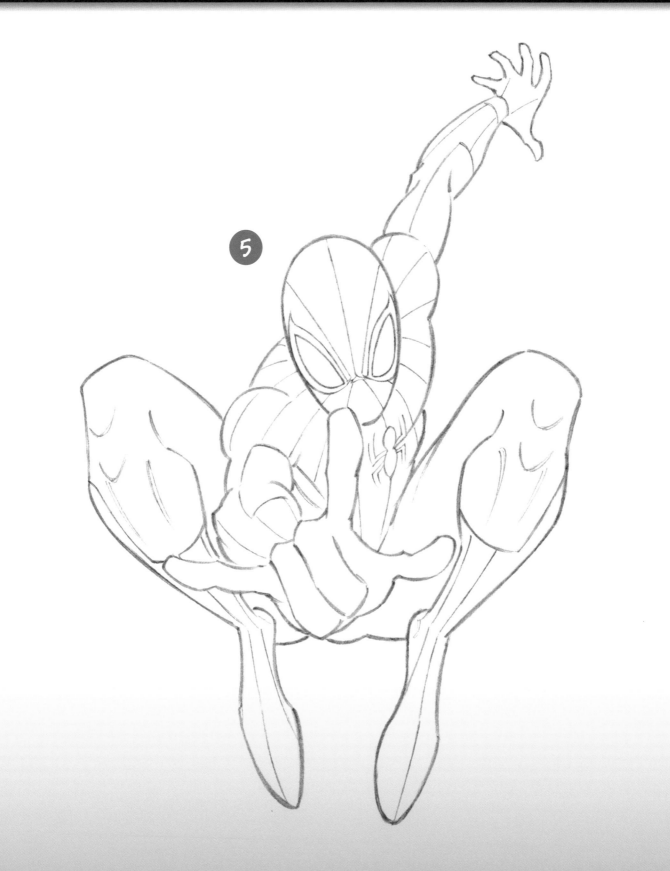

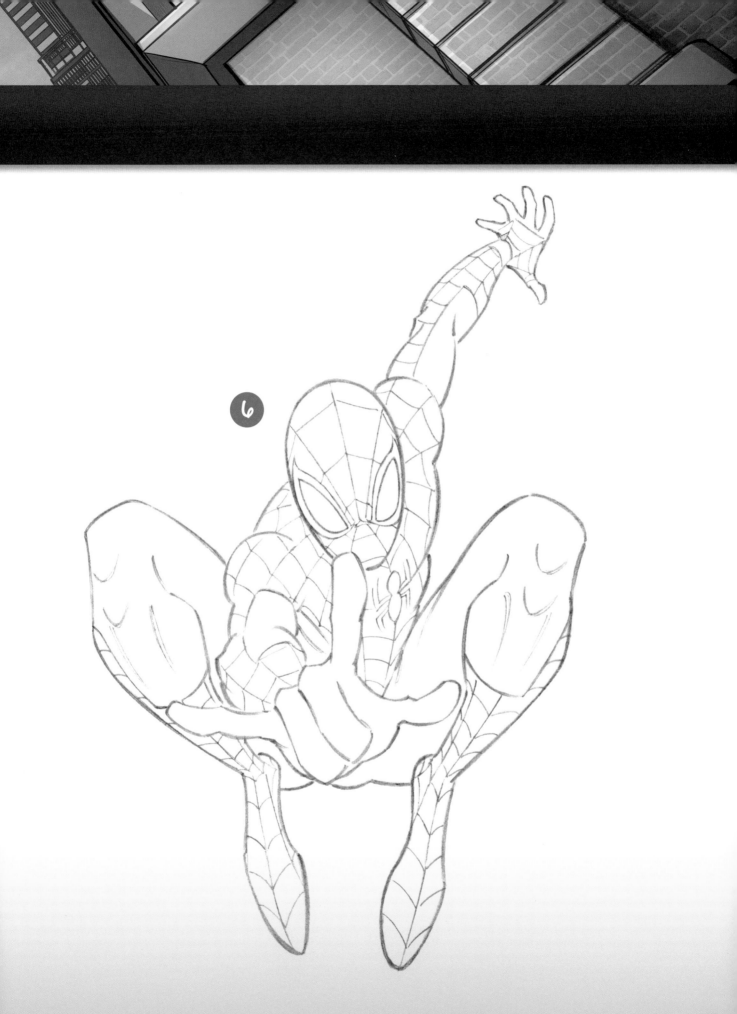

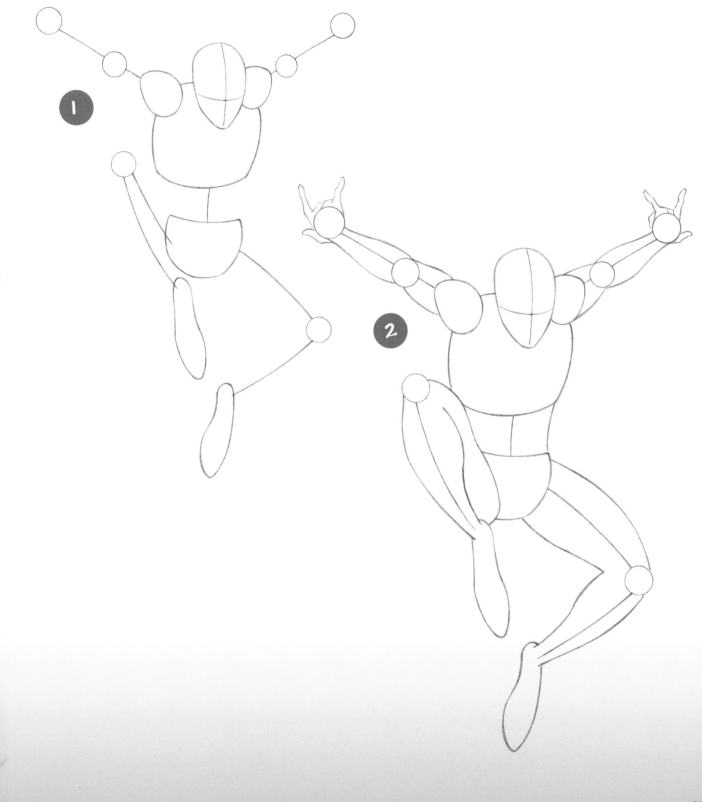

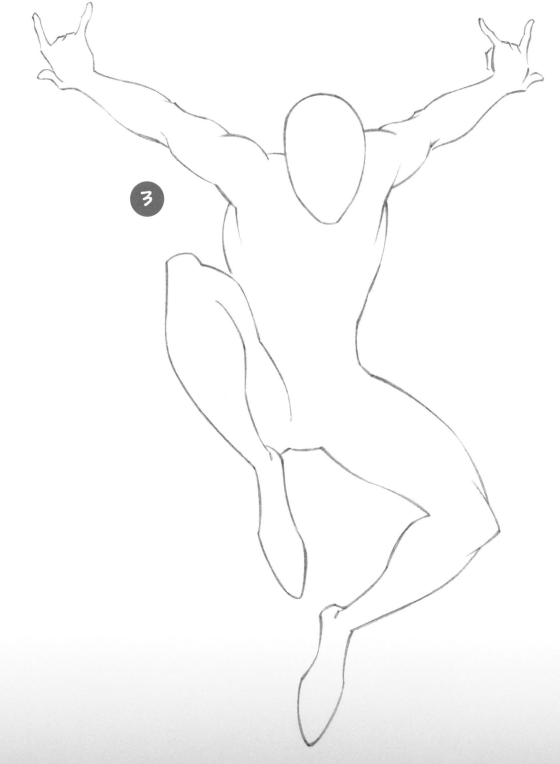

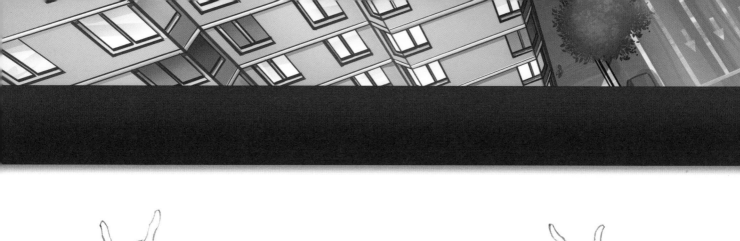

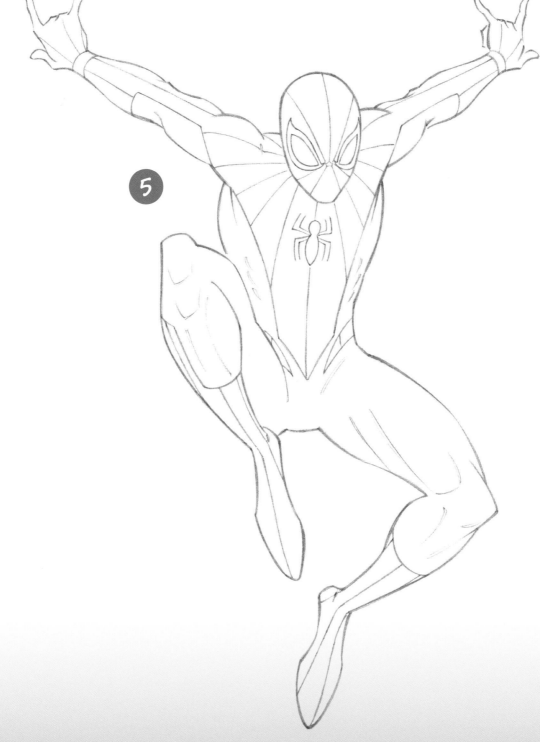

6

Originally priced at 13 cents, a near-mint copy (9.6 CGC) of *Amazing Fantasy* sold in 2011 for $1.1 million.

8

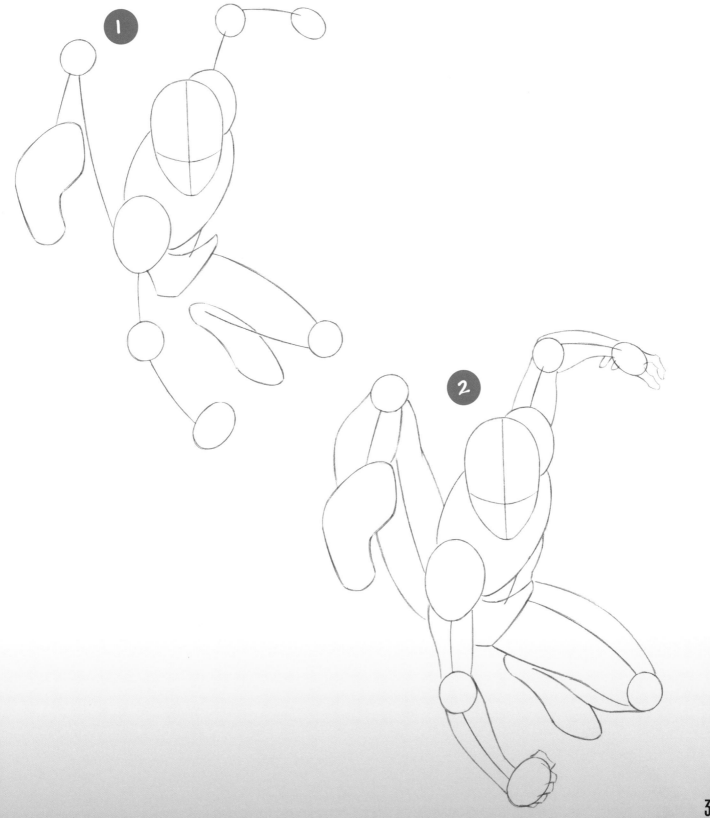

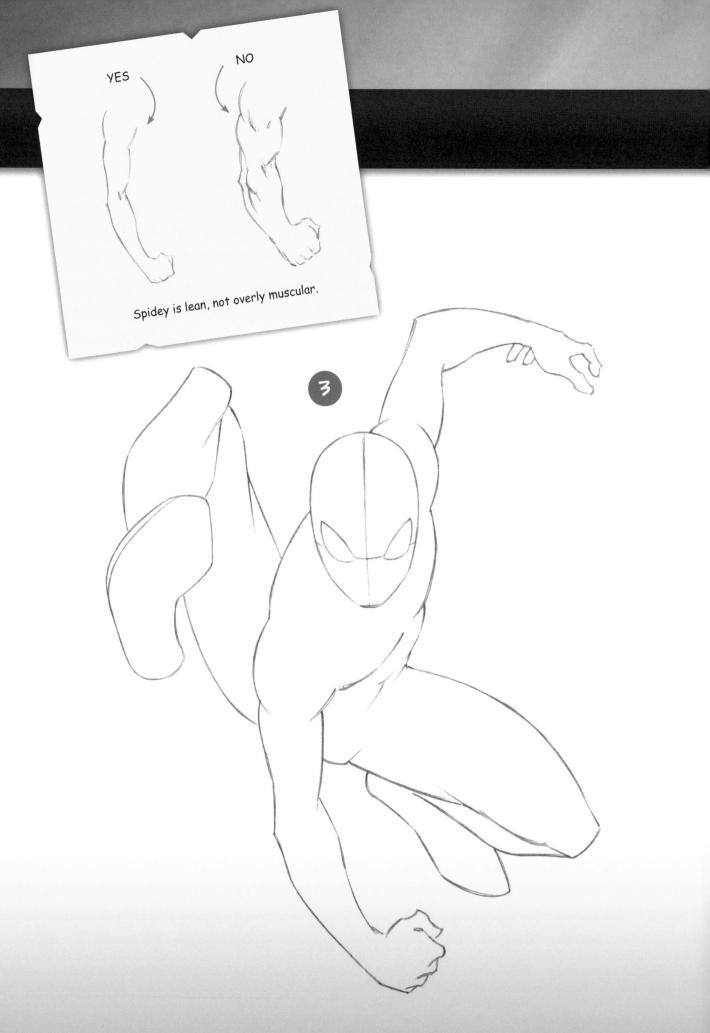

YES

NO

Spidey is lean, not overly muscular.

The Amazing Fantasy #15 issue was so popular that Spider-Man got his own comic book, *The Amazing Spider-Man*, in March 1963.

Use the eyes to convey emotion.

4

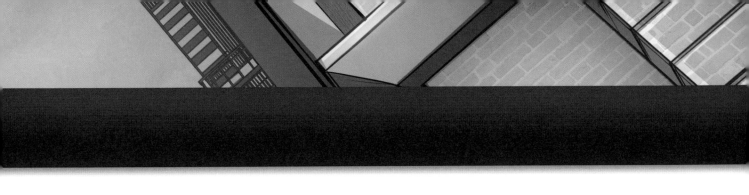

Spider-Man is Marvel's most popular Super Hero, probably because he is relatable to readers.

8

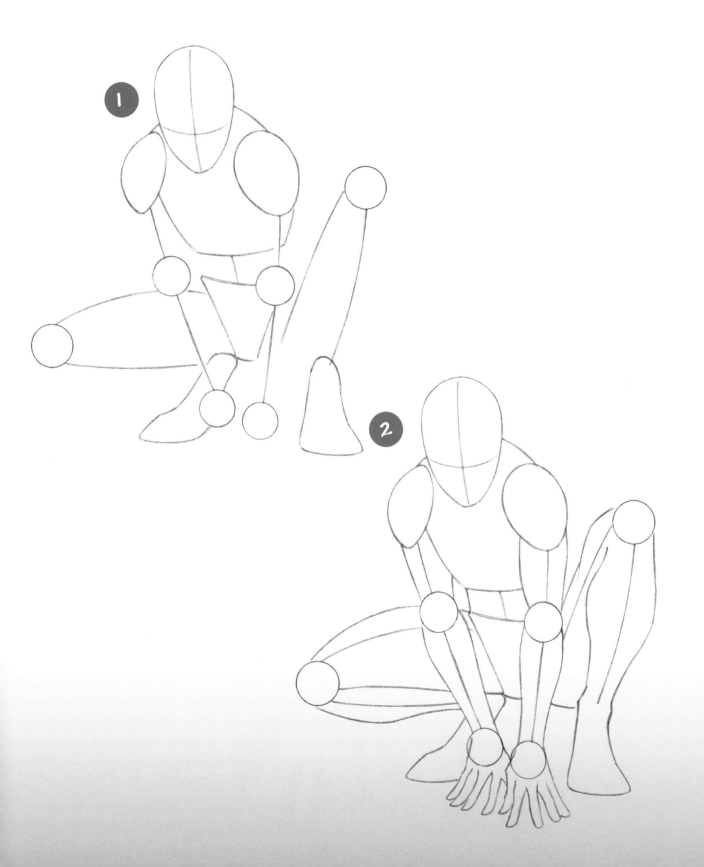

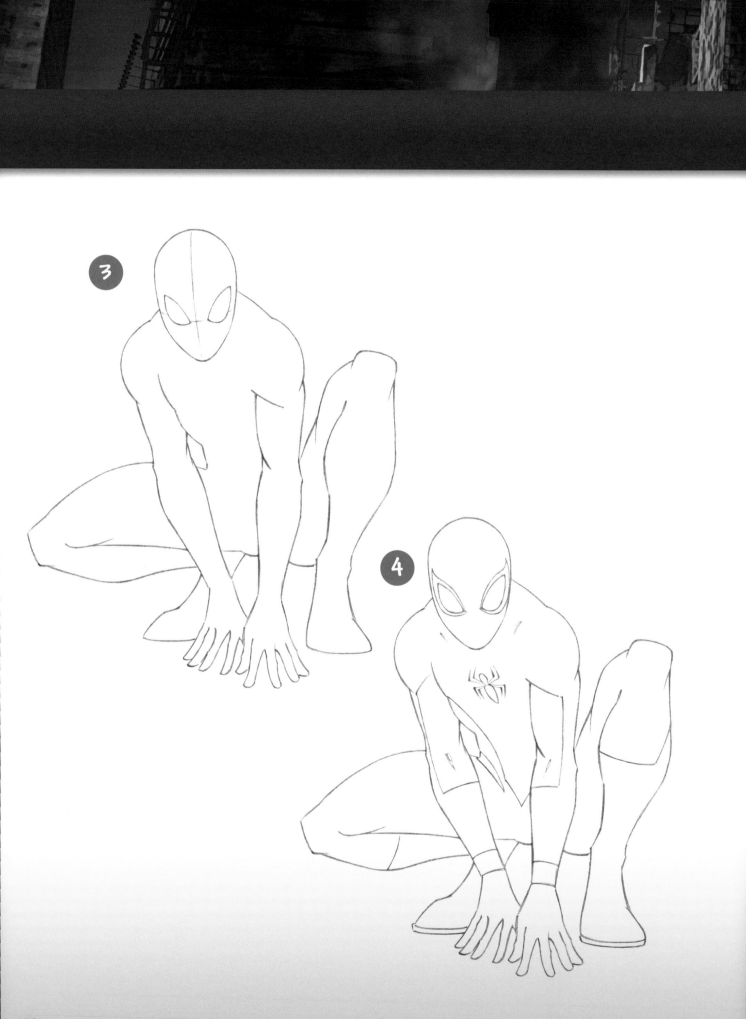

YES

NO

Spider-Man's chest

5

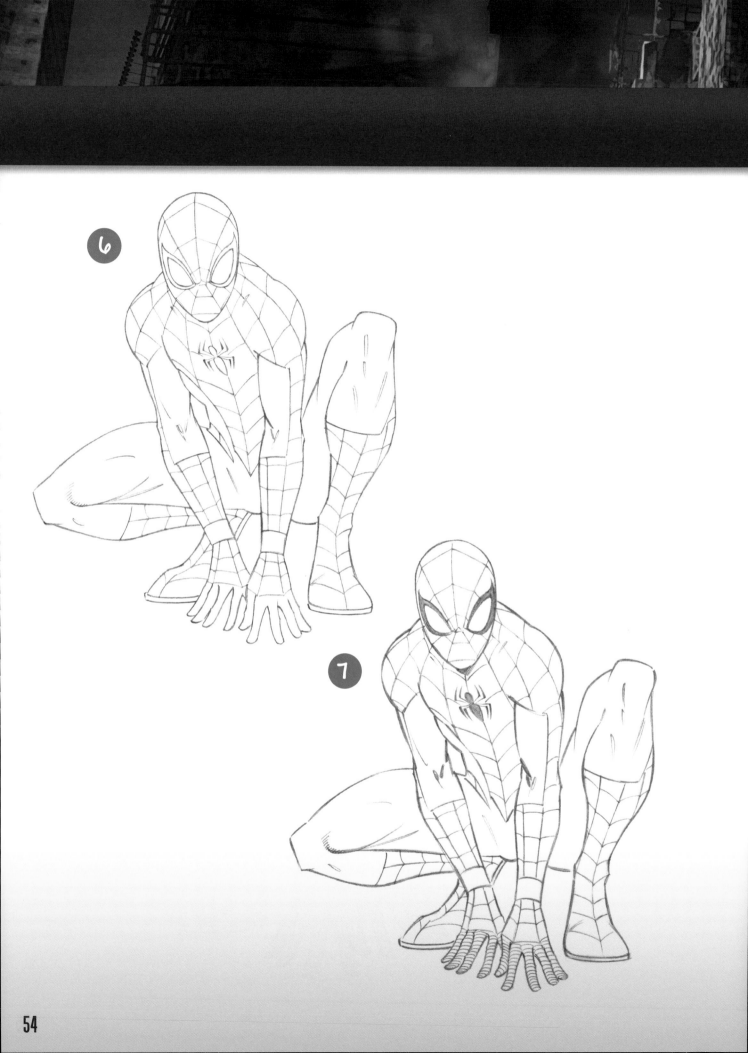

Spider-Man was the first teenage Super Hero that was not just a sidekick to an adult Super Hero.

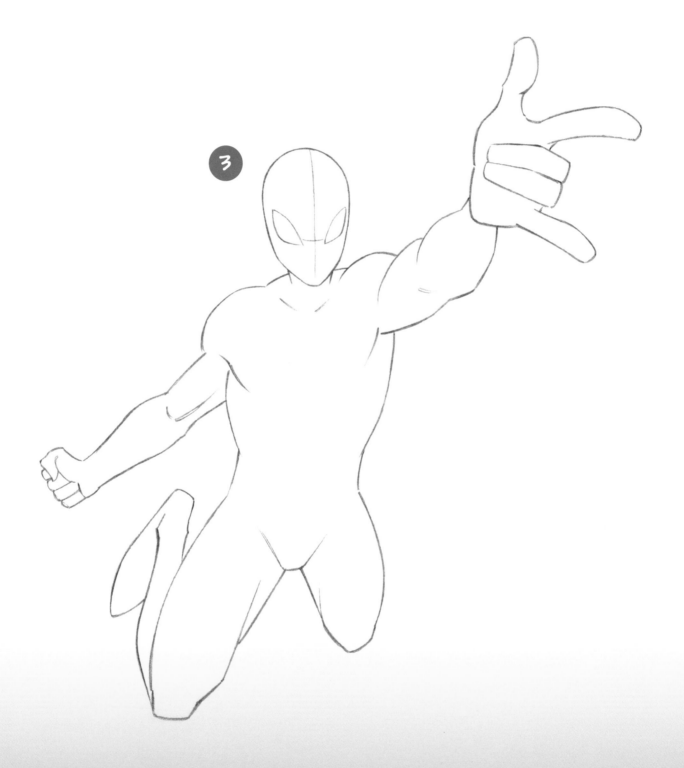

The *Amazing Spider-Man* #1 cover art was by Jack Kirby and Steve Ditko.

4

6

Spider-Man's webbing looks kind of like tangled-up spaghetti noodles.

Also available from Walter Foster Jr.

**Learn to Draw
Marvel Spider-Man
Villains**

ISBN: 978-1-60058-835-8

**Learn to Draw
Marvel Avengers:
Favorite Heroes Edition**

ISBN: 978-1-60058-828-0

**Learn to Draw
Marvel Avengers:
Mightiest Heroes Edition**

ISBN: 978-1-60058-829-7